LUSH

LUSH

Frazier Russell

Four Way Books
New York

Editorial Office
Four Way Books
PO Box 535
Village Station
New York, NY 10014
www.fourwaybooks.com

Library of Congress
Catalog Card Number: 00 134380

ISBN 1-884800-30-0

Cover Art: Anselm Kiefer, *Sefirot*, 1990-1991
Courtesy of the Marc and Livia Straus Collection
Book Design: Brunel

This book is manufactured in the United States of America and printed on acid-free paper.

Four Way Books is a division of Friends of Writers, Inc., a Vermont-based not-for-profit organization.
We are grateful for the assistance we receive from individual donors and private foundations.

ACKNOWLEDGMENTS

Poems from this book have appeared, some in different versions, in the following publications, to whom grateful acknowledgment is made:

American Letters & Commentary: "The Book of History"
The American Voice: "How We Are Saved" (appeared as "How We Are Spared")
Global City Review: "Photographs of Chester County, 1935," "Photograph of Frances Farmer"
Marlboro Review: "The Vessel"
Phoebe: "Prayer"
Ploughshares: "My Father, the Commander, Poolside at Fifty-Five"
Two Girls Review: "Mandelstam in Prison, Dreaming of Nadezhda"

For their responses to these poems in manuscript, my deepest thanks and love to Martha Rhodes, Pat Mangan, Eric Darton, Connie Lovatt, Elena Alexander, Stephanie Russell, and the members of the Thursday night class at The Writers Studio.

for my father, Captain Edgar Farr Russell, Jr. USN (Retired)
for my brother, Lieutenant Colonel Edgar Farr Russell, III, USAF
and for my wife, Stephanie, with love

and in memory of my mother, Jean Neely Peake Russell

Contents

II.

Prayer

There is a place where
it is always midnight.
Where the pond grows lovely
in spite of not being seen.
Where the one who is dying
is not dreaming, when his body
is showered with roses.

I want to tell you the day
is fast approaching when the famished
may sit down together
at the same table and eat.
When the hands of the beloved
will clear away the rubble
of the heart.

May this breast
be the place where
the tuning fork is struck.
Where what is bruised about the body
shall not crumble. Like the skeleton
of a tree when you touch it.
On this avalanche of evening
when the dead and living come together
what is despicable on earth shall topple.

1

Lord, admit
us, we lived here, almost happy, almost yours.

—Dave Smith

Wheeling

Driving the highway
in my Impala
with the power seats,
listening all night
to the good news
of the gospel stations.
Once in another life
I dreamed this dream:
eating collards
from a can
in the light rain
west of Wheeling.
Lit up phone booth
with its bullet holes
by the side
of the road
and the johnson
grass overgrown,
five milligrams
of diazepam
finally kicking in.
Happy to be
nowhere near
anywhere in particular
but the brute
choir of cloud
and power line
overhead.
Highway lit up
by my headlights,
white lines

like scotch tape
laid down
then lifted up
from the pavement.

The Accident and What Came After

It wasn't the doctor running
the eraser-end of a pencil
up the soles of my feet
to check for signs of paralysis.
But the elms mostly bare
as a prairie outside my window,
high up on Union Street
in the late October light.
What I remember most
of those days is the ordinary:
the sudden feel of fringe
on my bare feet from the carpet,
walking with my dishes
after lunch into the kitchen.
Lighting Linda's cigarette
in a doorway. Keeping
the flame going in the wind
as I walked the ten feet
towards her with a match.

Christ Unadorned

Not mere succulence but the plum
itself on a glass plate over there
under the skylight. Undertaking
the hugeness and what comes with it.
Like aspens high above Santa Fe
in the fall. Or Giacometti in his studio
refusing the easy truth by painting
only eyes and skull. Not wanting
to finish the face of Yanaihara.
More than mere desire day after day.
Not the cancer but mother and son
in the kitchen eating dinner in the quiet
of that house with the Schubert on.

Gospel

Supine on the sofa
this hump of summer night,
lupine outside,
listening low
to Miles's lush republic of trumpet
on *It Never Entered My Mind.*
Outside my window,
fireflies & clouds:
perfume by the bucket
in a five-and-dime sky.
& I am lucky enough I know,
black-eyed peas & peppers roasting on the stove
& Miles's horn punching its sweet puissant hole,
blowing nuance
with his thimbleful of notes,
eased like water from a dropper
this moon & ju-ju night
just me & my soul
like a Fuller Brush man
broke down on his way through the Badlands
& no one knows it.
Like Miles told:
it's all in the withholding.
What you don't give up
you get back ten-fold,
        so saith he of the bump & tongue—
        here endeth the Gospel.

Mandelstam in Prison, Dreaming of Nadezhda

And M. said: "stay awhile,
thou who didst
live a little in me
and then didst not."

Hope—nightbook
with its pages
like beaten wings.

Smell of her ass
in the air—
that only Heaven.

Elegy

Were he to come,
the one in whose hands
she nightly lay the page
of her white hair,
fanned out in his palms.

Alcohol

I pour a double and then its brother.
Four a.m. again, moonlight and a pool
of flop sweat accrues. We are dirty
this much is true, precious little other.
There is no loneliness quite like home.
How many a cappella dusks remain
for us? I want all the abundance back:
something sober, fine before the soul's
shudders set in. In winter late evening
at kitchen tables, drowned and out,
ashtrays overflowing and absent minds.
Say *thy, thine,* patting pockets for Luckys
while empties stand mute sentry.

East Texas Two-Step

That smell of whiskey
delicate as vellum

in the evening early.
Bruised fruit moon.

Loose bits of tobacco
on your tongue, O

breasts suddenly
from your bra

undone. Panties
down around your knees

in the front seat.
We pass a jug between us

like a disease.

Venice

It felt like someone's lips.
I heard the church-bells ring.
The bird in me was singing.
The sunlight and the smells
from the fish vendor's market.
It felt like someone's lips.
The glide was so delightful.
Picasso in his striped shirt painting.
I dreamed I was dying.
The dolphins too were friendly.
The mating call of me wall to wall.
The sucking sound was priceless.
Wittgenstein and Francis at Cambridge.
The lubricant is leaking.
Puccini on the phonograph plays.
Madame Butterfly in her make-up.
The light fine as a geisha leaving.

Drink Spilled at the Bar in Memory

When I think of him, it is always
Greece. Standing there strong in the sun.
In kimono and workboots. On a bluff
overlooking the bareness of ocean and after.
Head back and fists raised in the fire
and wind of beauty. Prospero
in his patience, despite the years
of banishment and betrayal. His eyes
wide. Magnificent in their managing.
And Gena in her white dress lovely.
The two of them dancing late that evening,
barefoot amidst the bounty of bleached stone
and sky that was their island. Steadfast.
Like oxen who would never leave Eden.

for John Cassavetes

Divorce

Then I repot the jade,
smell the water
in a vase of tulips
and know it needs changing.
The Gods in their kindness
give us the minutiae to hold onto
and the beauty.

Blue Tango

Say it's the year of their courtship,
your mother and father,
in the ballroom of the Shoreham Hotel,
summer 1952.

In this plush setting,
the orchestra swells
time and again to a tune
always their favorite.

Any Friday night you could find them
on the dance floor.
He in tux and cummerbund.
She in a black strapless,
hem brushing the waxed wood
as though it were a lilypad.

Surrounded on all sides by Jesuits
and their débutante dates
in crushed velvet,
pearls around their necks
like a load of light.

How you love to imagine
that somehow everyone in that room
although a little tipsy
will get home safely
and fumble in love for their beds.

That the smoke from cigarettes
ringing the room in red
like hot coals is still rising.

Say somewhere birds lift off the lake
and it never gets light.

From the Sudden Darkness

When he was a child sleep came to him gently, lulling him with the warmth of its ritual as each evening, beneath a pile of blankets, he reached over to turn off his beloved lamp and felt the light from it cast its warm net over hand and wrist. Moreover, he remembered the feel of the light chain between thumb and finger (like a small rosary), and how he ran his fingertip over each brass bead, counting them; and that chain clinking when at last he pulled it; and how for what seemed like minutes, but was only seconds after the light in his bedroom had been extinguished in favor of a sovereign darkness, he could still see the shape of that lamp and its white shade, as well as the furniture of his room, here the night table and dresser—pulsing with an even more brilliant light now that they were consigned to darkness or what appeared to be darkness but which was like a mist clearing as the boy lay in bed with his eyes open, waiting for the furniture to bloom in full form from the sudden darkness, the cup full of pencils on the table now becoming clear—arriving almost like guests in their heavy coats all at once for a party.

Still Life

Who would know them? Seated
side by side on the porch,
old age with a drink by its feet
attending youth in crisp khakis,
their knees nearly touching.
Fireflies like a porchlight
coming on. Out front, pin-oaks,
the smoke from both their
cigarettes. And the father
who turns his chair away
while his son is still busy talking.

Montrose Park, 1962

There was the park in August
and the bellies of the boys
on monkey bars swinging like kings
back and forth, in their crewcuts
flat as Nebraska. And their mothers
in hats and gloves seated on benches,
leaning close at tea-time talking
tennis, willows overhead,
and the sickly boy whose name
I never knew in a sailor suit
who sat mute in his patch of shade.
And Father in his crisp civvies
at sundown with a cigarette
chasing me into the maze.

I Am in Love with Vicky but Cannot Confide in Her Until the Voice Says It's All Right

Each day the voice lets me get
as far as her back gate,
where I stand at dusk looking

into her dining room, where
Vicky now is setting the table—
knife and napkin—so delicately.

Even the ant I saw crawl
across her right knee during
recess last week, I love.

I imagine her dainty white socks
laid out on her bed—orchids—
the night before—and her black

patent leather Mary Janes
on the floor at her feet
like me sleeping. I have seen

her father polishing them
on his knees in her bedroom
late when no one's looking.

In the backyard with her telescope,
I imagine the world, holding
still for her—like me in my pj's

to watch. And for a minute, the sky
a black bowl turned suddenly over,
and the wind a canyon that keeps on coming,

and Vicky and me in our underpants only
standing up to our mouths in the sea.

My Father, the Commander, Poolside at Fifty-Five

Think of him all that summer
at poolside, in seersucker shorts
a size too big
and a sombrero,
hoisting highballs—
a few past a few too many—
in memory of his Men. His "boodies."

Or floating in the pool, say, with swimfins,
his body, bird's-nest frail
after surgery, the stitches running
like the Yangtze River
down his chest
Krazy Kat in all directions.

Not once but twice
when the wind blew his toupee
to the table, "I am not a failure,"
he said.

To top it off,
a toga party
at which no one showed.
Only his bony shoulders like a boy's
in the dim light, his gaze
a bulb suddenly gone out.

Child Falling from the Top of a Slide

Happy cross on a hill I am,
nothing the wind can bend, atop
the shiny slide in the sun, arms
outstretched, even autumn is ant
to me; the boys and girls: my congress
of birds below, and papa and mama
pointing, in hats; and I am spinning,
the shorts like sacks around my spindly
legs, and elms, elms everywhere.

Balthazar

I am thinking tonight about the death of my donkey Balthazar,
whom I baptized with creek water when I was nine:
Balthazar for whom there is no beginning or end
tonight as I remember him.
And I am nine again riding the little cart he pulled with hay
on the way to market.
Balthazar in whose hair we wove garlands
the afternoon of our first communion;
and how that day while I was churning ice cream
I ran barefoot to be beside him,
and the sheep shaded him high up on the hill in the grass
and would not at first let me in,
and how as he knelt down slowly
on one knee then the other;
and I laid my forehead against his,
felt his fur and heat,
Eden of this earth and its other;
my arms wrapped around his neck;
and there was his breath on my wrist
fly on his eye, his stomach moving in and out
and the grass stiff as pencils, hard dirt underneath
and there was only the sound of the bells of the many
and the men on their tractors in the distance
and Nannie Craig ringing the bell out front for supper
as though it were any other day.

Charity

The children
from the
elementary
school
outside
our
window
each morning,
playing
Ode
to Joy
patiently
on untuned pianos.
Smell of
French-roast
coffee
from
take-out
cups
on the table.
Not to mention
a slice
of Valencia orange
left out
on a plate
from the
night before,
its fragrance
all but spent
like a wick.
Half-moon
of my fingernail.

Reading Chekhov
or not.
You on this
first morning
of spring,
hair pulled back
in a ponytail,
barefoot
with the breakfast
bowls
in the kitchen,
gold paint
lightly applied
to your toenails.
Your blue bath-towel
where you left it—
still wet
from the shower
on the back
of the rocking chair.
Abundance
in everything
like the word
wisteria.

In Winter

In a rooming house
at the absolute edge of town
where a middle-aged man
touches the tip
of a young boy's penis
lightly with a lit
cigarette
it is midnight.

And somewhere ice cracks
like a side of flesh
splitting in black wind.

And somewhere the stars—moth-holes
in the night sky.

My brother:
the shards of glass
embedded in your arms—
bright stars in a field of stubble.

To the young one you were:
a slim boy standing
at the edge of a field in winter
in your mother's white wedding dress,
urinating delicately
on a pile of leaves.

I give you the bare branches of a tree
tied with tiny ribbons
that blow slightly in the wind.
And silence that lays down lightly:
little girl
on the hood of a car in the rain to sleep.

The Book of History

It is forbidden to be old.
—Rabbi Nachman

I.

Think Lost, think Lick,
think Little-Poison-Heart.
And so the piles of spoons

and baby shoes—
and so the language
of scraped paint

lifted from the canvas—
luminous like Icarus
word after wounded

word. As if History,
the grave of the painting,
was about to happen:

in the pigment layered
like skin, like grafts,
like waves lapping the this

and the that—

II.

—As though the worst
that could be
had been done

to the meat
that had been her
already. History:

the gestural, in other words,
had happened,
arms of the dress pinned out

like a specimen
as if to say: *Lord,*
in this one's name—

III.

Like the boy
at the window
in his room

late one afternoon
in the town of____________,
or so the story is told.

Letting the nimble wind
finger the text
of him so delicately;—

holy, holy, holy,
page after page like a deer
in the clearing,

succumbing to the abundance
and the burning.
Wanting to bend over

and be entered
in the garden by the fists of meaning,
as though for once

he was what it wanted—

IV.

        And the Angel said:
Think Lost, think Lick,
        think Little-Poison-Heart—

for Anselm Kiefer

The Vessel

It's beside the point what his intention was,
        the artist

who naked nailed the head of his penis
        to a board

during a performance in San Francisco
        last summer.

Or for that matter, what the audience
        thought, seated

in a circle the second before hand
        and hammer,

the irrevocable, in other words, went down.
        I speak about

the meaning's meaning: the essence of hand,
        hammer and nail

to penis. Meaning not the shock attendant
        afterwards

or the instant before when the mind's mouth
        suddenly understood

its mortality. I speak of that place
        beyond feeling.

Not the Penitentes of Las Cruces
        who each Easter

chose one of their own to crucify
        on a hill overlooking

sand and shrub, in other words, the hereafter.
        But rather

the opera of mind and matter that is weather,
        the essence even

of intention when intention is emptied out.
        Like Francis Bacon's

painting of his lover, overdosed and alone
        at the end.

George Dyer dead, face down in the basin,
        his body naked

and misshapen. Bare bulb on a string
        overhead.

We are neither meat nor meaning.

What the Good Book Says

In my backyard again,
settled deep in the Adirondack,

          day's fandango
          at its end.

Neighbor's radio playing something
familiar by Bill Monroe,
from the kitchen in the distance.

Reading Augustine, Issa.
An inch of this, an inch of that.
Grass like a bad crew-cut on my bare feet.

          Under the fat shadow
          of the lone sycamore.
          Broken-down town of clouds above,
          slant light of summer

laid out for me
one last time
in its linen suit.

—

Wrist and hand:
those pale orchids
of the poor,
I once wrote
in the high prairie
and dry grass
of another life.

Meaning, I guess, just that.

—

Night highway ribboning out,
                                        white line, white line—
In the sky above,
                                        hawk moon diminished like a dime.

My fortieth year now come and gone.
Penciled in then penciled out
like the road through Barstow.
It's said there are those
among us who know, though
I'm not one of them,
fingering my beads,
my daily portion, as I do.
The roll-call of the nameless goes on.

                                        Lock-step of language and landscape

I attend to.

And tell me where it is written
we were meant for more?
Busted note of wind and pin-oak.
And dusk with its tin cup
at the back door.

2

But it is not only their bodies but their postures that I know, and their weight on the bed or on the floor, so that I lie down inside each one as if exhausted in a bed, and I become not my own shape and weight and self, but that of each of them, the whole of it, sunken in sleep like stones; so that I know almost the dreams they will not remember, and the soul and body of each of these seven, and of all of them together in this room in sleep, as if they were music I were hearing, each voice in relation to all the others, and all audible, singly, and as one organism, and a music that cannot be communicated: and thus they lie in this silence, and rest.

—James Agee,
Let Us Now Praise Famous Men

Photographs of Chester County, 1935

Not the father and son
        walking hip-deep
into the cotton fields
        with shotguns.

        But dusk
a busted thing that abides
        on the back of the water moccasin.

There is the world we are given
and the one we learn to live in—

        —sweet syllable of the soybean,
        word like a whump of wind—

Here is a red schoolhouse
its ghost vocables
deepening into evening;

        and a girl waiting by a fence
        for her grandfather in a hat on horseback

in the slack wind of Christmas,
the back of Chester County broken.

        Sweet Jesus, there is a river rising
        in all of us—

Even an inch of ant parts the grass—

How They Lived

In torn dresses mended Sunday for school,
boys and girls in blue jeans, barefoot,
on the dirt road to school. Some on bicycles,
some walking. Children of field hands and farmers.
And Saturdays at the soda fountain drinking lemonade,
eating patty melts and reading the funnies,
the picture shows and pimento sandwiches.
For Christmas BB guns bought on lay-away.
Babies bathed and given hot toddies.
God's a locket and water moccasins.
Naps at noon and matinees.
Evenings on the porch,
soft glow of the radio dial in the dark.
Back of the hand and bed,
dreams of the dead walking in wheat.

You Shall Know Them

And the sun outside going down slowly like a bowl covering the immense bitten sky; and the thistle and weed outside the cabin knowing not and cowering not. And all the creatures of this place: cottonmouth and jay, oblivious as the first crackle of flames licked, kiss-like up the sides of the walls; and even then she scarcely moved, but lay down dove-like, quiet as cotton on the swept wooden floor, at first out of fear, as though stillness would render her invisible to the flames, as though the mice in their quiet would come to her; and her hair spilling out along the floor. And she saw again the faces she had seen all the days and nights of her life, in the dusty rooms of Fishing Creek Church with its high windows and deep in the cotton fields, in light and dark, in waking and sleeping. And the fear then, as if it was suddenly a meager wave, ebbed all at once away from her and there was only she in that body and no door anymore, and the bounty of her flesh, *flesh that giveth and taketh*; and the crackle as the beams above began to pop then split; hot embers sparking off the oak above; and ember and beam and spark spoke to her: *Sister*. And all the things of this house, this life: dirt and dusk; and the pine floor planks beneath her began to heat and the robe of smoke now was like a great wind sucking out the air. And she could not open her mouth in the smoke, and now the sole and only light was the embers falling down on all sides of her like a sky full of stars in that cabin and the room was as a great candle flickering, and she an immobile and solitary figure in it; and the body that had been created in his image, suckled and cherished and savored, body that had seen birth and earth, and had laid to rest so many kin under hard dirt and delta, did not so much as move anymore but curled inwardly upon itself, ruminant; matter and mud it was not, smoke and shadow it had become; and the delicate wrists began to curl as though the body itself were becoming young again, pure again, a girl-child again, finger-printless and not part of this world any longer, and neither smoke nor flame could hear or harm her.

Stomping for Albert Ayler

Hallelujah
Mr. Hereafter:
Mr. Steampipe
stove pipe
pipe up
woe is the world
exeunt brother
in a pork pie
deliver me
settled deep
with the
good news
of dew and
grass blade.
Albert, Albert
the gut-bucket
heating duct
late night
rooming-house
tone
of your notes:
dirt laid down
on the stage.
At Slug's Saloon
your beautiful truth
like scrapple
and apple
frying
on the stove
O Albert,
for the last time
this poor fucking earth

and dirge
of your pilgrim wind
blended in
with trumpet and violins.
Albert: my landscape
brushstroke
and locus,
grass spongy
after rain
in the dusk
of these
last days.
Late autumn
elm and maple
bunched out there
bare
against the
immensity
in the dusk
of these last days
we play
what we're
given to play:
a heaven of crawdad
and immensity.
O dew
and grass blade
or so
the wise ones say
halfway to hallelujah
on alto
Albert knew
the Bayou truth:
out of absence
out of broken notes
and ash we issue.

Detail from the Life of Robert Johnson

Yonder: the horizon
like piano wire

and the *uh-huh*
that dusk is.

We all said.
We all did.

Barefoot,
just that

by the clothes-
line in a pine

chair
with a jug

of the good
stuff. Verily,

I say: wind stiff
as a wash tub.

Lesson

Rain on the roof like a bucket
of birdseed hurled

in a sudden gush of wind.
A scholar in his dark

armchair,
studying hair by hair,

a single page of Torah.
The argument of ankles

moving through timothy
out back.

Blues for Bud Powell

I write your name:
Bud at *Birdland*
your autumn stand
1953,
throwing down
a travelling blues
Un Poco Loco
like it was money
honey,
your blunt fingers
& buttercup touch,
vamping gent-elegant
at the piano,
all ruin & nuance.
Bud making like mercury
with the 88's,
cigarettes lit
& sucked like lips
right down to the tip.
Bud in the bye & bye
Goodbye Pork Pie
sweet lick & spotlit.
Before *Bloomdido* Bird
went down for the count.
Before the whiff of whiskey from an empty glass
    breakdown sound—O immense verdure
roundelay & yonder—Bud a dervish
mowing down notes at *Chat Qui Peche*
using your whole body,
the jellyroll of your soul;
all knuckle & elbow
nail-bitten skin begin again

before the glossolalia of days
& smack bled out in a bathroom haze
Brooklyn Bud
beautiful & solitary on the stage
if pain had a name:
—this your child Bud like an upright left out in the rain.

What I Remember of Driving Through Wichita at Night

The glow,
the station,
its rusted-out
oil barrel
by the pumps
and across
the road
through
the windows
of the diner
lights going
suddenly out and
the black after
where someone
his back to me
at a payphone
was perhaps
talking
or else waiting
out the wind
and rain
and the parking
lot deserted
but for
the last car
as I drove past
my windows up.

after Donald Justice

Abide, Abide

In the window
of a building
eight bricks
stacked
flush
all these years
just so
in the sunlight
the third
from the top
that one
with a white
chip in it

in memory of Donald Judd

My Friends

There's Jim at fifteen shooting hoops uptown
and Louise in her Armani evening gown.
Sad-eyed Edie in her Issey Miyake
and Connie on St. Mark's
her shaved head:
snow falling in a pot.

And Bill in organza with his hair
piled high by the piers;
and Sophie in her crib,
her tiny fists at two:
tulips in bright moonlight.

And now my friends are getting out
in their long coats by the lake,
in thigh-high boots and ballet slippers.
Evening eddies: a hymn at its end.

Angel Eyes

And I think I never
heard a touch so
light as his,
Jimmy suited up neat
with the brushes,
breezy as laundry
drying on the line.
And a buff-colored
fez on his shaven head,
playing *Angel Eyes*
on his drum kit
with a trio;
pocked skin of the snare
and the ride cymbal
he rarely rode
in the club
with the high
windows and a blast
of late afternoon light.
Yes, I remember him
with a hot plate
at the Palace Hotel
on the Bowery,
nodding in time
to Ellington's
Come Sunday
into the evening.
And the knack he had
for appearing
in his camel-hair
finery at night
out of nowhere;

thin as incense
on St. Mark's,
outfitted either
in white or black
linen depending
on the season,
detailed
down to the cufflinks.
Even the last name,
Lovelace, went down
smooth. "How you doin'?"
he would ask
under a fluttering
streetlight at daybreak,
smelling always of patchouli
as he palmed
a joint to you.

Gin, 1974

He was American, fat, addled
& middle-aged; in love with love:
that dull thud to the grave.
He who tipped the scales at 220
after bingeing on take-out
& Tanqueray. Later, listening
to the refrigerator,
in a party hat with a tub
of whipped cream. He is 31 again,
svelte, tipsy at a faculty tea,
unhooking undergraduate bra after bra
in the bushes with his teeth.
Nearer my nipple to thee,
he sings, his mouth that gorgeous
gash of red.

Entitled

At the Russian Tea Room he ate each Sunday.
He was eighteen and so deserved it.
Always beluga caviar and blinis.
Stolichnaya served in a block of ice.
Toodleloo is what his brainstem said.
The waiters in red coats did his bidding.
Jailbait and the famous filmmaker at the next table,
feeding her fois gras from his finger.
Her hiking her dress to reveal no panties.
All that year he lived the muted life of money,
clipping cigars in Southampton on the sundeck.

Away, Away

Blinds drawn, listening to *Sergio Mendes*
& Brasil '66. Empties in a paper bag
stowed in the closet next to his girlie mags.
His wife, what's-her-name? away, away.
Bits of last night's NoodleRoni,
snug in his beard—a snack for later.

Paradise

He dreams an alternative existence: his wife, bags packed,
on the train to Schenectady and mother. Waking to his new life
as a sunbeam, he parades the wood floors unbelted
in his drunk Otherness. *Is there more to life than meat*,
    he wonders,
puffing a Panatella. He pours himself a short one.
Paradise comes down to this: a dusk soft as carpet-slippers.

Booty

On the crapper we find him again
stomach distended. Face pasty
as a cleric's collar. These days,
alas, there's more of him
out than in—

Epitaph

That winter,
libido on the lam,
he worshipped subtlety
in the Proustian sentence.
Sonny-Boy his mama called him.
Praise to his flabby ass.
Day after day,
nothing whatsoever came to pass.

The Story of My Life

I was born I will die goodbye. Beware
cigarette burns in the upholstery.
The sky over yonder
bleached as a preacher's collar.
Thy tongue is mud and flea.
This is either a poem
or else it's a glass of water.
Lonely is as lonely does.
If there's a ditch half-way wet,
I'll stick my dick in it. Meanwhile,
summer's a coming,
the wind bitchslaps me.
Death tends its chickens.

How to Write a Poem

For example: the wind in the kitchen banging the pots hanging from hooks at dusk in summer. Fuck poetry and the horse she rode in on. I admit what I like is to watch a woman drink expeditiously a six-pack of beer and then squat. Right now, in my mind's eye, I am watching the stream come out of her down there in that hidden place that articulates her for me. I am not getting any younger—which is the message my wife, when she was still my wife, left on our answering machine, exactly one year ago to the day. The city I am writing this in is Omaha or at least I think it would be if I opened my eyes. Ice cubes melt on the table. This is just the type of detail I like to read when I read a story. I don't know about you, but I have all day to get this out and then some.

Marriage

What matters most is not the photograph
of them on their wedding day. Toasting
each other with champagne, the flutes
like France. Though they too at the beginning
are beautiful. She in her white slip
of a dress. He in tuxedo with a tartan
bow-tie. They stare at each other in profile,
smiling. Not love like orchids arranged prettily
on a plate. Or Brazilian friends preparing
their marriage bed at the hotel later.
But fierce love like tea master Rikyu's lesson to his student,
Hideyoshi, the shogun he summoned to witness
his imported morning-glories bloom. In Japan
the first ever of those flowers. Then proceeded to cut down
each one in the field outside his hut before
Hideyoshi arrived. Placed the last in a vase on the wall
for the ruler who traveled far and expected many
and in his rage at last was enlightened.
Meaning the man and woman
this and every autumn afterwards.
Learning to sit silently in their souls together.
Not abundance or severity but the steadiness between.

for Stephanie

Father Barbecuing at Thirty-Five

That fourth of July, out back,
we watched father flipping burgers

and talking Bay of Pigs. So fit
in Topsiders and madras shorts. He liked

us to call him "Commander" after
too many Dewars. That day

he sat naked in the bathroom,
cleaning his shotguns, one by one,

before the party. Later, after the neighbors
went home, Father in flip-flops

stood watch over the backyard with binoculars
'til the coals went cold. "Cadets,"

he called us that evening, in coonskin
caps and plastic hatchets. We never left our post.

Photograph of Frances Farmer

The mangled language
of her honey-blonde

hair is what I remember
and the mouth like Belfast.

Frances in handcuffs,
hauled drunk into the

police station late,
her feet at the cameras

kicking. Light like the law
on her face.

Fat night
like a bass player

getting it right.

Seven Years Later Saying Goodbye

The serious men on stools
in the bar that never closed.
The incense of piss in that place.
You and me playing pool with a pitcher.
Sailors in a booth nearby smoking.
Later, me driving drunk in the blue Camaro
with the headlights off up the hill
in the dark to your house in winter.
The stunned dove I was in those days
deciding whether to die. The smoke
in our clothes and hair after undressing
in the foyer. The foghorn of the ferry
outside your window. The ornament
of us that looked like love.

How We Are Saved

What I wouldn't do to say again
it's the night before you died. That somehow
I see you lying there in bed
before me now. In all your illness,
your body a bare Eden. I need you
to know I worship this last image
of you: all bones, an orchard
of evening without end. I need you
to know, your body tucked in tight
is holy to me in hospital sheets.
That your sex beached to one side
of your thigh is beautiful. That I would
heal you if I could. Listen:
I'd summon up the dead and living,
the oily tides of the Ohio to lay on hands
and bless your black lungs.
To kiss disease right out of you
with rapture. I'd tell you that someplace
in central Texas, nuns since 1900
pray for you. That even the stutters
of the dumb tonight are silk.
I need you to believe in the essential
beauty of Sophie, Marie and Lucie whose hair
is surrender and has the power to heal.
I need you to believe I'm Christ
in your kitchen, riding backwards
on a donkey. That somehow, somewhere
I could give you back your life
one last time. Grandfather, my presidency
of light tonight! I need you to believe
I'm you in white tie and tails. The bouquet
your bride Ida threw and you caught at the beginning.

Alcohol Tritina

O marvelous first sips from a bevelled glass, it is the envoy
  of evening;
tingle of Cuervo Gold on my tongue and snug that winter,
muffled in the plunge of red couch, warmth in my young sex
      never ending.

Loneliness of a porchlight coming on in winter;
and the distant sound of a bossa nova dying down from the
neighbor's bungalow never ending.
Smoke and topiary: night: children hunkered down in sleep:
      my sweet leaves all that evening.

Night is the page buried in snow, let my dead help me now,
  never ending.
Night an ant on my wrist. I am the angel *bueno*. Night comes
  in its pants and doesn't
know it so, *Mi Corazón*, my eyelids flutter, *Mi Stephanie*,
  this evening.
A small boat bumped loose from the kiss of its dock, O night
  and elm
      of sentence in winter.

I take thy world on my tongue and suck; it is winter
  and evening
      like this sentence is ending.

But

But there is another world
where the dead jostle in their graves
and the damp grass is heavy as love.
Where a child in kneepants
plays jacks by a fountain
which inexplicably turns on
one day at dusk.
And the town-crier
rubs the sleep from his eyes,
poised with an accordion
against the horizon.
Who am I?
No-one's rose
or a sick man like a gate the wind blows open?

Afterword by Philip Schultz

A number of years ago Frazier Russell came into my poetry workshop at The Writers Studio; he was energetic, passionate and obsessed with poetry and everything surrounding it; all in all he was noticeable. I soon learned that his poetry was also noticeable. He casually dropped the names of obscure French poets I spent entire nights trying to familiarize myself with, and in the end, as in all such relationships, I learned a great deal. It's rare to meet someone as devoted to the art. Devotion is the word too, for the poems of *Lush* are all about various states of devotion.

There are many admirable qualities in this debut performance that are noteworthy: devotion to craft, idea and feeling; an honest and respectful sense of the tradition he is joining ranks with, with the proper amount of reverence given—but the fact of the matter is, like it or not, one's foot taps while reading these poems. At first one thinks it has something to do with their seriousness, their almost reckless determination to go after something not quite within reach; that perhaps one is responding to their vision or the spirit of adventure that is found in each poem; but no, it is the music of the language. The sheer music of it. Finally, what we have here is music; literally. Frazier Russell loves language and jazz and he's smart enough to give us both.

I think of Michael S. Harper and Yusef Komunyakaa and what they have done for poetry by giving it such a purely American sound. Russell gives us Bud Powell's *Un Poco Loco* and Ellington's *Come Sunday* and Miles's "lush republic of trumpet/on *It Never Entered My Mind.*" He gives us "whiffs of whiskey" and "immense verdure" and "nail-bitten skin" and "upright left out in the rain" and "camel-hair finery" and Mandelstam in Prison and Wichita at Night and "bump and tongue" and a good many prayers. In fact, what the music is all about, finally is prayer. He gives and he gives and then he gives a little bit more. That is his art; that is what language and music are all about in the Gospel according to Frazier Russell: "all ruin & nuance." Amen!

Frazier Russell is a core faculty member of The Writers Studio, a private school for writers located in Manhattan. He has given readings and conducted workshops at numerous venues including Lincoln Center, Cleveland State University, The Detroit Opera House, The Knitting Factory, the Hudson Valley Writers Guild, and the St. Mark's Poetry Project. In 1996 his chapbook novella, *Fweivel: The Day Will Come* was published by Ridgeway Press. He is also the author of a biography of Ernest Hemingway for young adults (*Ernest Hemingway: Romantic Adventurer*, Kipling Press, 1988). His poems and book reviews have appeared in *American Letters & Commentary, The American Voice, Global City Review, Marlboro Review, Phoebe, Ploughshares,* and *Two Girls Review.* From 1992 to 1997, he served on the Board of Governors for the New York Foundation for the Arts. Currently, he serves on the Board of Directors of the Mad Alex Arts Foundation. He lives with his wife Stephanie, an artist, writer, and cultural activist, in Brooklyn, New York.